Salty Irina

Eve Leigh

methuen | drama

LONDON • NEW YORK • OXFORD • NEW DELHI • SYDNEY

METHUEN DRAMA
Bloomsbury Publishing Plc
50 Bedford Square, London, WC1B 3DP, UK
1385 Broadway, New York, NY 10018, USA
29 Earlsfort Terrace, Dublin 2, Ireland

BLOOMSBURY, METHUEN DRAMA and the Methuen
Drama logo are trademarks of Bloomsbury Publishing Plc

First published in Great Britain 2023

Cover design: Paines Plough & Broccoli Arts

Cover image © Eve Allin, Stef Felton and Emily Cosaitis

A catalogue record for this book is available from the British Library.

A catalog record for this book is available from the Library of Congress.

ISBN: PB: 978-1-3504-3538-4
ePDF: 978-1-3504-3539-1
eBook: 978-1-3504-3540-7

Series: Modern Plays

Typeset by Mark Heslington Ltd, Scarborough, North Yorkshire

To find out more about our authors and books visit
www.bloomsbury.com and sign up for our newsletters.

Salty Irina

For B.

Thanks to: my family. Jessica Stewart. Eve Allin. Salome Wagaine. Debbie Hannan. Yasemin Özdemir, Hannah van der Westhuysen, and Francesca Knight. Broccoli Arts. Paines Plough. Callan McCarthy and everyone at Methuen Drama. Anthony Simpson-Pike. Emily Aboud. Sarah Grochala. Guy Jones. Louise Stephens. Nadia Clifford, Serena Manteghi, and Olivia Morgan. Owen Calvert-Lyons. Suzanne Bell. Chloe Smith. Everyone who read for the Bruntwood Prize in 2019. Juliana Taralezova. Tassos Stevens. Moritz Sauer. Thekla Neuss. Jasmine Lee-Jones. Henning Bochert. Nick Hytner. Simon Stephens. Mariame Kaba. Daisaku Ikeda.

Specifically no thanks to Paul Scholes, a horrible cat who tried to delete this playtext many times.

Two people speak.

Anna *is from the south.*

Eireni *is from the north.*

There is a third woman present, **Jana**, *who acts as an assistant stage manager on cans before she joins the action. She helps them with the props; she helps them tell the story. She's the audience's friend onstage, until she's not.*

/ denotes overlapping dialogue.

. . . is a thought the speaker cannot finish.

– is a pivot of thought.

(text in brackets) is not spoken aloud. When it comes at the end of a line, the speaker wants to say it but is not able to.

In general, punctuation and line breaks reflect rhythms of thought and speech, rather than grammar.

& The Canoe (Story Films/ITV), *Teju's Tale* (Short – Sky Arts/ DBK Studios), *The Girl Before* (42/HBO Max/BBC), *The Outlaws* (BBC/Big Talk Stephen Merchant).

Creative Team

Writer – Eve Leigh

Eve Leigh is an award-winning, internationally recognised writer working across theatre, screen, games, installation and digital art. Works include *Midnight Movie*, which premiered at the Royal Court Theatre and was selected for the Berlin Theatertreffen Stückemarkt 2020; *Wildfire Road*, which premiered at Sheffield Theatres in 2023; *Salty Irina*, shortlisted for the Bruntwood Prize 2019 from 2,561 anonymous submissions; and *The Trick*, which debuted at the Bush Theatre, followed by a national tour produced by HighTide Theatre. She leads the first-ever Royal Court/ Deafinitely Theatre writers' group for Deaf writers. She was joint Jerwood/Royal Court New Playwright 2019, and the first-ever Artist in Residence for the Experimental Stage of the National Theatre of Greece in 2017.

Director – Debbie Hannan

Debbie Hannan develops and directs new work for stage and screen, having trained at the Royal Conservatoire of Scotland and as Trainee Director at the Royal Court. They are currently Associate Director at National Theatre of Scotland. Previously they held the positions of Acting Artistic Director of Stockroom, Associate Director at the The Bunker Theatre and Incoming Artistic Director of the Traverse Theatre, Edinburgh.

Recent theatre credits include: *Faun* (Cardboard Citizens, Alphabetti and Theatre503), *Sound of the Underground* (Royal Court), *The Panopticon*, *Exodus* (National Theatre Scotland), *The Strange Undoing of Prudencia Hart* (Royal Exchange), *Overflow* (Bush Theatre), *Constellations* as Associate Director

Cast

ANNA
Hannah van der Westhuysen

Theatre credits include: *An Enemy of the People*, *Henrik Ibsen* (Here Now Ensemble), *After Troy* (Andromache Platform Theatre), *Naked Not Nude* (Vally Neuzil Platform Theatre), *Lunch Hour* (Southwark Playhouse), *Lipstick & Scones* (Liz Venture Wolf @ Leicester Square Theatre).

TV and film credits include: *Sexy Beast* (Paramount+), *Sandman* (Netflix), *Fate: The Winx Club Saga* (Netflix), *Lamborghini* (AMBI Distribution), *The Bay of Silence* (September Film), *Sleeping Arrangements* (Jog Road), *Grantchester* (Kudos).

EIRENI
Yasemin Özdemir

Theatre credits include: *You Bury Me* (Paines Plough/Bristol Old Vic/Royal Lyceum Edinburgh/Orange Tree Theatre), *Angel* (Edinburgh Fringe/Tour), *Dance to the Bone* (Sherman Theatre), *Living Newspaper* (Royal Court), *We Need to Talk About Grief* (Donmar Warehouse), *Romeo and Juliet* (Frantic Assembly/NYTW).

TV and film credits include: *A Spy Among Friends* (ITVX), *Yummy Mummy* (DreamMore Films Ltd), *Patrick* (Auntie Margaret Productions), *Vandullz* (BBC Sesh/BBC Wales).

JANA
Francesca Knight

Theatre credits include: *A Streetcar Named Desire* (Almeida Theatre and West End), *Lear's Daughters* (Creation Theatre), *Witness for the Prosecution* (County Hall), *Julie* (National Theatre), *E15* (Lung Theatre/Edinburgh Festival/tour).

TV and film credits include: *Obsession* (Hartley Pictures/Netflix), *The Suspect* (World Productions), *The Thief, His Wife*

Sound Design Associate – Annie May Fletcher

Annie is a Yorkshire-based sound designer and composer. She was nominated for a WhatsOnStage Award 2023, shortlisted for the Evening Standard Future Theatre Fund 2021 and was the 2018–19 Laboratory Sound Designer at Nuffield Southampton Theatres.

Theatre credits include: *Accidental Death of an Anarchist* (Theatre Royal Haymarket/Lyric Hammersmith/Sheffield Theatres), *Hope Has a Happy Meal* (Royal Court), *A Passionate Woman* (Leeds Playhouse), *Splintered* (Soho Theatre), *The Odyssey: The Cyclops* (CAST, Doncaster), *Brilliant Jerks* (Southwark Playhouse), *Children of the Night* (CAST, Doncaster), *A Christmas Carol* (Bolton Octagon), *The Beauty Queen of Leenane* (Theatre by the Lake), *Rock* (Sheffield Crucible), *Hedwig and the Angry Inch* (Leeds Playhouse/HOME Mcr), *An Adventure* (Bolton Octagon), *Endurance* (Battersea Arts Centre/HOME Mcr), *Autopilot* (Pleasance, Edinburgh), *The Survivors' Guide to Living* (Manchester Royal Exchange), *Some People Feel the Rain* (The Den – Manchester Royal Exchange), *Decades* (Leeds Playhouse), *The Understudy Live* (Palace Theatre).

Associate credits include: *Carousel* (Regent's Park Open Air Theatre), *Enough* (Traverse Theatre), *How Not To Drown* (Glasgow Tron, Lawrence Batley Theatre), *The Audience* (Nuffield Southampton Theatres).

Costumer and Design Consultant – Sophia Khan

Sophia is an experienced Wardrobe Supervisor, WHAM (Wig, Hair And Makeup artist), afro hair consultant and facilitator. She started her creative career working as a dresser and then Wardrobe HOD for live music shows, working with bands and musicians from George Michael to Lady Gaga, and from Dolly Parton to Motorhead, before venturing into the ice-skating industry, touring globally with a variety of different live shows and subsequently moving into theatre. In recent years she has held workshops

(Donmar Warehouse & Eleanor Lloyd). Film includes: *Mo <3 Kyrah* (Film4).

Lighting Designer – Laura Howard

Laura trained at LAMDA as a recipient of the William and Katherine Longman Charitable Trust Scholarship.

Assistant Lighting Designer credits include: *Amadigi* (ETO), *Constellations* (Donmar/West End).

Lighting Designer credits include: *Invisible* (Bush Theatre/59E59 Theaters), *Faun* (Cardboard Citizens), *The Beach House* (Park 90), *The Kola Nut Does Not Speak English*, *Elephant* and *Clutch* (Bush Theatre), *Manorism* (Southbank Centre), *Exodus* (National Theatre Scotland), *Dead Air* (Stockroom), *Dismissed*, *Juniper & Jules*, *Splintered* and *curious* (Soho Theatre).

Composer and Sound Designer – Alexandra Faye Braithwaite

Theatre credits include: *Falkland Sound* (RSC), *Sound of the Underground* and *Purple Snowflakes and Titty Wanks* (Royal Court), *Cat on a Hot Tin Roof*, *Bloody Elle*, *Wuthering Heights* and *Light Falls* (Royal Exchange Theatre), *The Narcissist* and *Never Have I Ever* (Chichester Festival Theatre), *Things of Dry Hours* (Young Vic), *The Wonderful World of Dissocia*, *Shining City*, *Room* and *How Not To Drown* (Theatre Royal Stratford East), *The Good Person of Szechwan*, *Anna Karenina*, *Operation Crucible* and *Chicken Soup* (Sheffield Theatres), *Groan Ups* (Mischief Theatre/Vaudeville Theatre/UK tour), *My Name Is Rachel Corrie* (Al Madina Theatre, Beirut), *Cougar*, *The Rolling Stone* and *Dealing with Clair* (Orange Tree Theatre), *Toast*, *How Not To Drown* and *Enough* (Traverse Theatre), *When I Am Queen* (The Almeida).

Broccoli Arts

Broccoli was founded by Salome Wagaine in 2019 and is now led by Eve Allin. The company creates work primarily for, by and about lesbian, bisexual and queer women and non-binary people. Broccoli most recently produced *Before I Was a Bear* (★ ★ ★ ★ ★ *The Stage*) which had a sell-out run at Soho Upstairs in June 2022.

Broccoli exists to produce work that has variety, ingenuity and relevance. They encourage queer writers and creatives to make work that is not defined solely by identity. They aim to create sustainability, opportunity and success for queer creatives and their stories.

Thistle & Rose Arts

Thistle and Rose Arts is a female-led, commercial theatre-producing firm operating in London and across the UK and Ireland. They make small- to mid-scale plays and musicals by, for and about women and non-binary people. The stories we tell combine the personal with the political, exploring identity and advocating social change. They particularly love to make work set throughout history and which incorporates folk themes. In addition to their commercial producing work, they also offer mentorship and opportunities for people of any age who are interested in theatre producing and early career professional producers.

teaching The History and Importance of Afro hair in TV, theatre and film. She is also a WHAM consultant specialising in afro hair and deeper skin tones, holding workshops for sound and lighting departments.

Production Manager – Ethan Hudson

Ethan Hudson is an engineer, production manager and eco-technologist who is interested in using new and old technologies to enhance live performance, create public space and pursue climate justice. His theatre specialisms are in site-specific performance infrastructures, sound engineering and special effects. He works primarily as a production manager for theatre, dance and large-scale participatory events. Ethan founded Frontseat Media, an equipment rental and technical services company in 2012.

Stage Manager – Daisy Francis-Bryden

Daisy is a freelance Stage Manager who has extensive experience in London's theatre scene. Graduating in 2021, they have worked on various productions as both a Stage Manager and Assistant Stage Manager. Theatre credits include: *Musical Theatre Showcase* (Mountview Drama School), *PLAYAI* (Riverside Studios), *Farm Hall* (Jermyn Street Theatre and Theatre Royal Bath), *Who's Holiday* (HOME and Southwark Playhouse), *UK Drill Project* (Barbican), *Horse-Play* (Riverside Studios), *Man in the Moon* (St Paul's Church and Belcombe Court), *Originals: Live at Riverside Studios* (Riverside Studios), *Orlando* (Jermyn Street Theatre), *The Night Woman* (The Other Palace), *On the Line* (London tour), *Footfalls and Rockaby* (Jermyn Street Theatre and Theatre Royal Bath), *GirlPlay* (Camden People's Theatre), *The Duration* (Omnibus Theatre).

Eireni OK, so.

You went to the city for university.

You're part of a vulnerable group – you're gay, but not just gay, your gender presentation is unconventional and that's how you like it.

You're very beautiful – I should say – you're conspicuously beautiful and your gender presentation is unconventional, which is something I've noticed fascists and homophobes tend to find especially provocative.

Your grandfather HATES that you've decided to come to this city for university – it had a bad reputation during Communist times, he says the city's full of Nazis.

He was worried about you coming here.

But you weren't.

I think that's a funny thing about being gay, it's not like being Turkish or Jewish or something, you can be the only one. In your family.

So you can feel like your grandpa is over-protective, but other people can feel like you have a victim complex or something, whereas if everyone's

'the same'

in the family,

maybe you don't all agree on how to handle it,

but everyone knows the score.

There's something amazing about you, I can't describe it any other way,

you're waterproof, any horrible behaviour or whatever just rolls off you –

I feel like I'm talking too much, you say something.

////

Anna   Er . . .

Fuck! I don't know.

You speak more languages than me.

You're from, the North, you're from a small town by the Baltic coast.

You . . . I like your . . .

I like the way you talk, it's like reading a book.

I like how you move when you think I'm not watching you.

Eireni *is a bit staggered and shy.*

Eireni   You don't need to –

please don't feel like you need to just compliment me.

Anna   I know. I don't.

Keep talking, keep talking.

////

Eireni   It's,

er,

it's cheap to live in the city compared to where you're from. You immediately find a family – of course you do – in an anarchist squat. (There are always loads of squats in cities with far-right activity.)

And then. It starts.

Because there's a murder round the corner from the squat, a murder of a tailor. They think he might have been part of the mafia. The mafia for some reason are always linked to particular immigrant groups – the Russian Mafia, the Chinese Mafia.

The tailor was from Senegal.

There is no Senegalese Mafia.

In the squat, you suggest that it might be a right-wing attack.

The others point out that southerners like you are always seeing Nazi interference in what is often the ordinary flow of local politics. You feel very young and very stupid.

Anna   OK no no no. I've got it. So you came to uni here because it's the biggest uni in the area, a bunch of your friends from home came as well.

'Friends.'

Eireni   They were friends!

They were basically friends, at the time they were friends.

Anna   They were the other nerds at your school, basically, and you don't actually have loads in common with them other than that you were pretty unhappy together in the same place at the same time.

Everyone at school called you 'the girl that never talks', and I wonder –

if it's OK to wonder this –

how much of that was due to the fact that you and your brothers were the only kids in the whole school who weren't white.

Cause fuck. You talk enough now you're here.

Your essays are stupid good. Your name stands out, it's unusual, it sounds Greek.

Eireni   Such condescending fucks, to speak to you that way.

Because saying that, that you're a Southerner, Nazi-hunting in the North –

You feel that your privileged point of view, your prejudice, has been exposed. You stay away from the squat for a while.

You think about the shipping pallets on the roof, about the grime of the city settling in the grain, about building a sauna.

And you know you need to go back to the squat before it's too late, before it'll be too strange for them to see you again, before it moves from being a slight embarrassment – OK, an intense embarrassment, but very – you know – not actually a big deal –

You don't want it to get weird.

But you don't want to go back.

And then there's another murder, of a Lebanese shopkeeper and his son.

////

Anna   Because your name sounds sort of Greek – your first name – people assume you're Greek sometimes. When you explain that you're not, some people just leave it at that. But honestly, not many people. Most people seem to think you owe them some kind of explanation.

This might not be true in other parts of the world. But here in northern Europe it is.

Sometimes you explain that your father is a minister, that your name means something like peace, or meant that to the early Christians. But that's not really the explanation they're looking for.

Sometimes you just want to keep it short so you tell them what they really want to know. That your father's from here but your mum is a Turkish Christian, which is a thing to be, she and her family came here when she was young. That they run kind of an unusual ministry in your small town on the coast.

And then they leave you alone.

OK let's be honest what they were asking you is your race, but they didn't want to say that. What they were saying is: I can tell by looking at you that this place will never be your home, so tell me where home is.

Which tells us nothing other than that they don't know what home means or how a home is built.

Them just being like HEY DID YOU THINK I WAS STUPID

WELL I AM STUPID

DEFINITELY

NOW YOU KNOW FOR SURE.

Sometimes you think the love between your parents is so absorbing that you'll never fall in love,

not never fall in love,

that somehow they love each other SO much, out into the Church and the wider world, you feel like you can only have a generalised love for other people, an unfocused love like the love of Christ, you've never had a best friend, you've never fallen in love, their love is such a bright colour that all other loves seem a little faded.

Eireni   That isn't true.

Anna   It is though.

Eireni   It actually isn't, though, it's really not, I have no idea why you'd say that.

The love of Christ isn't fuzzy or – unfocused.

It's,

for some people,

it's the strongest thing,

they can feel themselves sitting in the hand of God.

Or –

. . .

Anna   I'm sorry.

Eireni   You make it sound –

Anna   I'm sorry, I didn't mean to, I'm sorry.

. . .

What would you like me to –

Eireni   OK.

Anna   Really.

What would you like me to say.

////

Eireni   You come back to the squat the evening of the murders, the word hasn't got out, everyone's happy to see you and it feels like,

you feel silly,

you felt like something big happened between you and the group and maybe nobody else felt that way.

But late in the evening the word comes through, same neighbourhood, same demographic –

Anna   Not the same demographic.

Eireni   What?

Anna   Not the same demographic, the tailor was Senegalese, the shopkeeper was Lebanese, and his son.

Eireni   No, but –

Anna   Senegal is in West Africa, Lebanon is in Lebanon, you're only off by a continent.

. . .

I am sorry, I said I was sorry.

Eireni   I said OK.

I meant, that they were both lower-middle-class immigrants, small business owners, in the same neighbourhood, executed in cold blood.

Anna   And his son.

Eireni   And his son. Yes. Which is why the police tried to say it was the, er, Lebanese mafia.

Anna   Even though, we've established, Lebanon and Senegal are actually pretty far apart.

And we might think – to make it explicit –

Eireni   I don't want to make it explicit, I don't want to, I'm so tired.

Anna   Why would the police make a link to the Lebanese Mafia . . .

Eireni   Maybe there's evidence we don't know about.

Anna   Or maybe they don't really care, maybe it's just not a high priority. To figure it out.

Beat.

Eireni   One of my least favourite things is when people bring up racist violence as if it has no emotional weight, at all.

Anna   We don't know if it's racist violence.

Eireni   You are making it explicit that it might be.

In some families the thought of – really bad things happening to you, because of your ethnicity,

it's like saying the name of the devil.

We know he's close, don't say his name, he might turn up.

White radicals talk sometimes like they don't mind if the devil turns up.

Beat.

Anna   I'm really sorry.

Anna *waits for* **Eireni** *to say it's ok.*

Eireni *knows that's what* **Anna** *is waiting for.*

Eireni   No, I just –

sometimes my,

back gets up,

when it feels like people are talking about danger,

and you just know it's not your danger, it's not your danger you're talking about.

Anna   . . .

Yes.

Yes. I see that.

Your danger *is* very frightening to me. The thought of something happening to you –

Eireni   I know –

Anna   I don't want you to feel like I'm just – counting bodies.

I don't want to count bodies.

Eireni   You're not, you're not.

Anna   . . .

Eireni   You know right away. You know it's not the – Lebanese mafia. Or the – Senegalese mafia. And this time the others in the squat are starting to pay attention.

Anna   How would we –

No, it's mad.

It's mad.

Eireni   What, they say.

Anna   If we could – stop it. If we could just make them STOP.

How would that work?

////

Anna   It wasn't such a big new idea or anything.

Eireni   Bash the fash.

Anna   We did it at demos and stuff.

Eireni   But it.

What if.

If there was a, serial killer or a,

Anna   'Serial killer'

Eireni   A,

'sequential,

murderer,'

whatever, who is murdering nonwhite immigrants and their children in *this* city, I mean, do you trust the police to deal with it?

Anna   Many people would not trust the police to deal with it.

Eireni   Many people note that the police use paid informers among the far right. Many people think that's just a way of funnelling money to the far right without asking for much in return.

Anna   Many people note that sometimes immigrants are beaten up by the police themselves.

But. Some people in the squat feel this is jumping the gun.

Eireni   Some people in the squat are suspicious of a teenage lesbian who seems to want to insert herself into what feels like a very grim situation.

Anna   I start building the sauna.

Eireni   Nicely uncontroversial.

Anna   You are doing – what, about then?

Eireni   I'm smoking. The window is open, it's a warm night.

Anna   The window is open.

Eireni   You're on the roof making a start on the sauna.

Anna   It's a yurt shape, relatively easy. But it's hard breaking apart the pallets without breaking the pallets themselves, the wood isn't good, the nails are twisted and vicious.

Eireni   You were hoping to recycle the nails but you found you couldn't.

Anna   Your window is open.

Eireni   I'm listening to Dolly Parton, obviously, she's my fave.

Anna   You're listening to Dolly Parton and you're thinking about the essay you have to write, which is about art and industrial decline in Great Britain.

You hear something.

Eireni   . . .

Anna   You hear –

Eireni   Nothing.

Anna   You hear a funny,

it's not screaming or,

it's not a scary sound,

you just notice, late in the night, that there is a bit of a different sound in the street

Eireni   I don't 'notice', it's not – it's like –

Anna   It's a bit of a feeling, a bit of a – 'what is that?'

Eireni (*hindsight – if only –*)   But I don't check.

Jana *pours water on the floor, slowly, quietly.*

Anna   You don't really notice anything at all until you leave to go to the shop on the corner at around dawn, for cigarettes and milk.

Eireni   And I step right in it.

Anna   I didn't know that.

Eireni   Yeah. I step right in it. And then I see.

And then I jump back onto the threshold.

My mother always said I'd leave the house without my head if it wasn't bolted on, she's right, how could I not have –

Anna   Because it didn't sound like you were expecting.

It never sounds like you think it's gonna sound.

The light of dawn is lurid and horrible, as always.

There's a lot of blood on the pavement.

Eireni   A bit of it on the threshold, now. Some of it on my shoes. I want to burn my shoes, but I don't have any others, so I just have to wear these with blood on them until the soles wear away which is disgusting, it's a disgusting thing to think right now.

Anna   There isn't a trail of blood. No footsteps leading away.

Eireni   So someone has bled profusely on the pavement and been carried away.

Has someone had a baby?

I don't know why, I don't know why I would think that right now . . .

Anna   The pavement, from the threshold to the gutter, is drenched in lightly clotting blood. It's probably about a metre square, a bit more maybe.

Eireni   I would say a metre and a half.

Anna   Someone has had the shit beat out of them and then been carried off. And no one has called the police.

Eireni   I should call the police.

Anna   But someone else might have called the police.

Eireni   Or maybe it's bad to call the police, maybe I'll be getting the wrong person in trouble, you know how the police are.

Anna   No crime scene tape, no one around. Just blood covering a space much bigger than any human body. In the quiet dawn of the city.

You don't think about the shootings.

Eireni   I don't know about the shootings right now.

Anna   To get to the shop, you're suddenly aware, you'll have to do a little hop to the bit of pavement with no blood on it then walk in a kind of big semicircle into the gutter, then around the bus stop and back onto the pavement again.

Eireni   That or walk through the blood.

Anna   You take off your shoes and walk backward into the hall.

You run upstairs and that's when you call the police.

It's getting warmer, you feel like you can smell the blood from your room, it's like a butcher shop.

You really need a cigarette. And milk.

You probably need a sleep but you can't.

Eireni   Adrenaline.

Anna   The heat of the morning coming on.

You lie on your bed and feel sweat prickle out your back. You think you might be sick.

Eireni   No sirens.

Anna   You're listening now.

Eireni   I'm listening with my whole body, I'm waiting for wailing or – sirens or –

Anna   Breaking glass –

Eireni   Something, and then I do hear something, and it turns out to be a municipal worker spraying the blood from the pavement.

Jana *starts to wipe up the water.*

Anna   You run downstairs.

Eireni   The light is very bright.

Anna   As you're putting on your bloodstained shoes, sitting on the threshold, you ask the man what he thinks he's doing.

Eireni   This is a crime scene!

Anna   It's about 7am at this point, the city is waking up, the roads are getting busy.

The municipal worker says they've taken samples, they've taken photographs, they have all they need.

And you are silent and look at him.

This is a busy road, he adds. People will need to cross through here.

And when you still don't say anything he goes back to spraying the gore into the gutter.

They are silent.

Anna   You sit on the threshold.

As people start to go to work you shift to one side, to the edge of the doorframe under the buzzers.

You don't like the sun but you absolutely cannot move.

At some point you start crying.

Eireni   And out of nowhere there's this voice.

Anna   Are you OK?

Are you – is there anything I can do to help?

Eireni   It's fine.

And you don't say anything. But you keep looking at me.

. . .

I could do with a cigarette.

Anna   I'll get you a cigarette.

Eireni   And before I know it she's gone, off in the direction of the shop on the corner.

////

Anna   I was expecting – I dunno. Heartbreak. Bad medical news.

When you told me what had happened –

Eireni   You came back with cigarettes, cigarettes and milky coffee, it was like I'd been under a spell for the past few hours and you'd broken it. You didn't act like you had anywhere to be.

Anna   I missed a lab session.

Eireni   When I finished the coffee I thought about going back upstairs to sleep but I realised I couldn't do that.

Anna   Adrenaline.

Eireni   Or just – it's too normal, to go to sleep. Not that it does anyone any good to stay up but just seeing something like that – something like that happening, literally on your doorstep – and just, going to sleep again –

Anna   You asked me if I wanted to walk with you. And I did.

Eireni   We went down to the river and saw all the buildings that had been rebuilt after the war.

Anna   I like to throw things into the river to see how fast the current moves. Leaves and sticks and, you know, not like chocolate wrappers or

Eireni   condoms or

Anna   I don't use condoms anyway.

Eireni   Really?!

Anna   Yeah I'm a lesbian. Dental dams or nothing.

Eireni   Clingfilm or nothing!

Anna   What?

Eireni   Don't you guys,

don't you,

use clingfilm or –

(*She makes a licking-clingfilm gesture.*)

Beat.

Anna   You feel like a hick idiot. Which you are.

I stole some croissants last night, do you want them?

Or not stole.

It was in the tip behind the Lidl, the packet was all sealed.

Eireni   Yeah.

Anna   And we sit and eat croissants in the sun.

Eireni   Where is the person who bled so much? What are they doing now?

Anna   Maybe being taken care of. By people who care about them.

Eireni   Maybe they're dead.

Anna   Maybe they're in hospital, are you sure –

Eireni   The police hadn't heard anything about it, I'm sure they would have done if someone called an ambulance.

There wasn't an ambulance.

I would have heard an ambulance.

Anna   Maybe they're asleep.

Eireni   And when you say that it's like a magic word, the croissant, the hot unreality of the morning makes me melt like spun sugar.

Anna   Let's get you home. Do you have enough food in the house? Do you have – everything that you need?

You look at me.

Eireni   You're rolling the edge of the croissant packaging tight and you do this little twist to make sure it doesn't unroll – I've never seen anyone twist the edge of a packet like that before –

Anna   You're still looking at me.

Eireni   And I just realise I'm not sure I've ever met anyone with the same

ability to manipulate the touchable world –

as you.

Anna   We walk back to yours through the old town.

Eireni   Out of nowhere, it grabs me, I think I want to ask you to come up.

Anna   You don't ask me to come up.

Eireni   You lace your fingertips lightly through mine but you've turned, you're walking away, you've already left.

Anna   You shout – where can I find you?

Eireni   You tell me the address of the squat.

Anna   We are looking at each other from either side of the place where the blood was, we're a bit too far apart.

Eireni   And that's when you shout – we have a sauna there!

////

Eireni   In my room with the shades closed against the sun, I think some more about whoever it is that bled all over the pavement.

Anna   Your mother has taught you that it's important to leave at the right time and go to the right place.

Eireni   No. She didn't –

Anna   She didn't teach you yeah she just told you the story, again and again, about how they felt the walls closing in, about how little by little they saw the country changing and at just the right moment they got out, your grandfather got a job in this country and took you all here, that's why it's important to know many languages to a high standard, it gives you more options, she waited for you to notice –

Eireni   she didn't scare us.

Anna   No I know.

I know.

But telling that story again and again, picking the right moment, and going – and never coming back –

Eireni   Papa doesn't like her telling us things like this.

Anna   She waited for you to notice that one day you might have to leave. As she had to leave.

Eireni   And we did notice that.

Anna   And you think about the blood and the disappeared body. I told you about the murders by the river.

Eireni   This is the city, this is the biggest city in my home region, it's supposed to be better here.

I think about your graceful hands, your narrow back. In the sun.

Anna   You need to sleep.

Eireni   Adrenaline.

Or –

Anna   I never miss classes but I was up late building the sauna, and I've promised you an actual working sauna now, so I head back to the squat and climb up on the roof.

Eireni   You work alone. You look out over the city – hazy in the heat, the cross on the cathedral bright gold, shining across the city.

Anna   The work is still slow. The nails are fucked.

Eireni   Right at that time, further down the river, towards the forest, other yurts are going up.

Anna   I break for lunch at almost the same time as them, probably. It's hot. The sun shines down on us the same.

Eireni   Preparations for the festival are well underway.

Anna   But we don't know that yet.

Eireni   Not yet. Soon.

////

A romantic song plays – 'Love Tastes Like Strawberries' by Miriam Makeba. They listen.

Eireni   I have strange dreams.

Anna   Of course.

I do too.

Eireni   Mine are about things that should be places but aren't places, missing papers, missing bodies in childhood beds, it's summer and it's too hot and people aren't staying in their beds, they're disappearing.

Anna   Mine are about digging in the garden with my grandfather in the south. We dig in the vegetable patch and we dig up something terrible, he doesn't let me look, he sends me away and I try to look but just before I see it, I wake up.

I sleep at the squat. I don't want to go back to my accommodation in case you come.

Eireni   You know I'm coming.

Anna   I know for sure.

Eireni   That's very arrogant.

Anna   I'm not saying I'm so wonderful or whatever but I know you're coming. I can feel it.

Eireni   I've never felt that way about anyone.

I've never felt sure like that. About anyone.

Beat.

Anna   Well you should try it, it's a great feeling.

Eireni   The sun is setting over the city and the starlings take to the sky. They've been hiding all day but when the sun starts to go down the sky fills with starlings.

Anna   Eating mosquitoes and such.

Eireni   Is that why they do it?

Anna   Yeah.

Eireni   I'm walking to the squat.

Anna   I'm going up to the roof again to work on the sauna. I'm so absorbed I don't notice you coming up and staring at me.

Eireni   I just want to see how long it takes before you notice me.

Fucking ages it turns out.

So I stand really close to you but you're still really absorbed in your work.

So I breathe on your neck.

Anna   Weird choice!

Eireni   Very weird choice, I regret that, wow.

And then you turn around.

Anna   You're so close. I didn't expect you to be so close. When I felt your breath on my neck I expected it to be anyone but you.

I should kiss you.

Eireni   You don't kiss me.

Anna   I don't know why, I panicked, I didn't expect you!

And it's so stupid

because here you are again

because you greeted me by weirdly breathing on my neck

but I think about that clingfilm thing and I –

. . .

Eireni   What?

Anna   I don't want to date queer virgins.

Or –

It's not experience, sorry, it's actually just I don't want to date people who –

I just need,

I'm not an experiment.

Eireni   And when you speak to me there's a little chill in your voice and I suddenly feel like I misunderstood something, the morning or –

I wonder what the fuck I'm doing here.

Anna   Do you believe in God?

Eireni   What?

Anna   I'm asking.

I'm just asking.

Eireni   . . .

I used to.

I used to be, really into it.

I would write my favourite Bible quotes on my trainers?

Anna   Wow.

Eireni   But now I'm –

confused about it.

I don't know.

I don't know.

Anna   Do your parents know that you might not believe in God anymore?

Eireni   No.

We don't talk about it.

Anna   You don't talk about God, in a minister's family?

Eireni   I think we just,

I think they can't imagine us believing any different from them.

I don't think it'd help to talk, I think it'd just upset them.

And you're an atheist, right?

Anna   No.

I'm not a Christian. I've never taken communion, I've never even been baptised.

But I feel like, sometimes,

like do you ever feel like there's fishing line in the middle of your belly?

Eireni   Fishing line?

Anna   Like a little clear tug, pulling you towards – something?

I really feel that way, I really feel like I know, sometimes I just know what I need to do, I feel this little tug like a fish on a line, and it pulls me towards – whatever, it pulls me towards my future.

It's not God, that feels like, embarrassing to think that something as – stupid and small as that could be God.

But I'm not an atheist. No.

Eireni   And then the others are on the roof.

Anna   We should have talked about something sexier, while we were alone, while we were alone I wasn't sure about pushing forward but now that the others are here –

Eireni   They've brought up a boom box.

Anna   And beer.

Eireni   And wine.

Anna   And actually it feels like we could push forward, she's instantly at ease with the others, she's a little shy but basically all right, and there's something about her being here in a big group rather than alone that makes it feel –

Eireni   No one is looking at us.

Anna   No pressure.

Eireni   The stars are beginning to come out, there's music, city lights, I'm on this roof with a bunch of strangers and I think yes –

Anna   I think yes –

Eireni   This is everything I hoped my life would be like when I was a grownup, I am out of my small boring town –

Anna   I'm so far away from the dull spa town where I grew up –

Both   and I'm finally having adventures.

Eireni   You brush my hair out of my face and your fingers are warm, they're absolutely radiating heat –

Anna   From twisting nails out of wood.

Eireni   Like pavement, baking hot after sunset.

Anna   You tell the guys about the blood on the pavement, about the strange sound and the disappeared body.

Eireni   It's getting worse, someone says.

Anna   Everyone can see it's getting worse.

Eireni   There was another murder today.

Anna   Turkish (**Eireni** *reacts*), ran a telephone repair shop, shot point blank like the others.

Eireni   It's got to be funded by somebody, they're richer than they used to be, did you see they're having a festival this week in the hills?

Anna   I don't remember who says that.

Eireni   Me neither.

Anna   I wish I could remember.

Eireni   Me too.

Anna   I wish I could remember who started making fun of me about bashing the fash.

Eireni   I remember they made fun of you.

Anna   I'm the youngest.

Eireni   Also I think sometimes,

dunno,

you're a doer.

Who's building a sauna on the roof out of nowhere?

Plenty of people talk about that sort of thing, but you –

'You should go to the festival,' someone says.

'See what you can see.'

Anna   That seems like a stupid idea.

Eireni   'Why?

I'm just curious why.'

Anna   I've sunk two beers at this point, which obviously isn't loads but I'm buzzed.

Eireni   'You're from the south! Don't they love that? Won't they think you're like, a forest maiden or something?'

Anna   I'm not even *from* the forest.

I'm from the –

not all of the south is the forest!

Eireni   Everyone's staring now.

Anna 'I thought you said we needed to do something.

You're a girl.

They're not gonna fight you if you're a girl.'

Eireni I'll go.

Anna What?

Eireni Yeah. I'll go.

Do you want to go with me?

Anna (Why do you say that?

Eireni I don't know, I don't know.)

Anna I don't want to go but I want to go with you.

Eireni We'll look out for each other.

Anna We're girls so they won't fight us. We'll probably be the only girls there.

Eireni It'll be an adventure!

Anna Plus, we'll try and find out –

Eireni Not try. We have to find out –

Anna more about this series of attacks, who it was that got bashed in front of your house and where they are now.

Eireni Everyone suddenly gets really excited about this idea except one old punk –

Anna Jonasz.

Eireni He's like, are you stupid?

Anna Look at your hair! Look at your clothes!

Eireni Do you think this is a funfair?

Anna He keeps saying that.

But we get really –

Jonasz is cool and he knows what he's talking about.

But something about the way he says it –

Eireni   'Do you think this is a funfair?'

Anna   We look at each other and we know we're gonna prove him wrong.

Eireni   An old man who doesn't know how strong young women can be.

That's what he looks like to us and definitely to a few others, later in the kitchen one of them –

Anna   Fatima – she says ignore the old white guys, of course they're gonna think you can't do anything.

Eireni   She says we should do it, we have to do it.

Anna   People can't keep disappearing around us.

Eireni   Only one person disappeared.

Anna   That we know of. They cleared up the evidence quick enough.

There's something strange – isn't there? In the way that it can touch your neighbours –

Eireni   the Angel of Death, laying his fingers on certain households –

Anna   but pass you by.

Until

eventually, one day

it doesn't pass you by.

Eireni   Something no one has mentioned is that I'm not white.

And I wonder why, Jonasz kind of talked about how it's dangerous to be butch but –

do they think I'm white?

Anna   Something no one talks about is whether,

does she think she's white?

Maybe she is white, maybe she's Spanish or – Italian –

She doesn't seem to think it's a problem. For her to go to a far-right festival.

Eireni   They don't seem to think it's a problem for me to go to a far-right festival.

Anna   Nobody quite knows how to talk about it.

Eireni   If I was at home my mother would stop me. Papa – he'd go out of his mind if I even mentioned it.

Anna   I grab you at the edge of the kitchen.

We don't have to, you know.

You really don't have to.

I don't want to ask you where you're from.

Eireni   I'm *from* a small town in the northeast, you don't want to ask me my race.

Anna   Yes.

Correct. Yes.

. . .

I don't know how how we protect each other.

Eireni   You're butch, you're gonna be in worse trouble than me.

Anna   If you think it's safe –

Eireni   It's not safe, it's not safe anywhere, but I can't just sit and wait anymore I wanna do something.

Anna   You're on the other side of the doorframe.

I want to kiss you.

Eireni   You go in for a kiss just as the woman – Fatima – is leaving the kitchen and you wind up kind of leaning into her shoulder and then bobbing back.

You literally look like you've shit yourself, you look like you've just done some unspeakable horror.

Anna   You kiss me.

Silence.

Anna   I didn't think you would do that.

Eireni   Well I did. I am.

Anna   And you kiss me again. Your dark breath, the wine. The soft damp at the edge of your hairline. I smell burning somewhere, why do I smell burning?

Eireni   Let's disguise ourselves.

This week.

We'll find a way to pass. Find a way to disappear.

Clothes that look like fascist clothes. Hair that looks like fascist hair.

New names.

Anna   New names?

Eireni   They shouldn't be able to find us, after.

They shouldn't be able to recognise us.

Anna   You're right. Of course you're right.

Have you ever jumped over a bonfire?

Eireni   No.

Anna   We used to, in the summers, sometimes.

Maybe that will impress them.

Eireni   They'll love you, I know it.

Anna   They'll love – that you're so pretty.

((*God that was so awkward.*) AH!! FUCK!! WHY!!

So I kiss you again.)

Eireni   It feels just like kissing a boy. The best-shaven boy with the softest skin.

Anna   It feels like a stupid miracle.

////

Anna   Our second date, if you want to call it that, is after dinner, at a second-hand clothing store called Love Saves The Day.

Eireni   It's not far from the squat, not far from the site of the first murder.

Anna   You've plucked your eyebrows, I notice, really dramatically, maybe right-wing women pluck their eyebrows I guess.

Eireni   I've shaved my body hair.

Anna   Oh shit, right, I'm gonna have to shave my body hair.

Eireni   Maybe not!

Some of them are kind of hippies, right?

Anna   I don't think they're hippies.

Eireni   No, but –

anti-capitalist.

Pro-environment.

Anna   Don't think that means being chill about patriarchal beauty standards.

Eireni   I mean, whatever, do what you want.

It was kind of exciting, shaving. As a novelty.

Anna   Yeah?

Eireni   It kind of felt like,

dunno,

like I'm a seal or something.

Like I don't recognise myself.

Anna   Maybe it'd be fun to shave.

Eireni   How do Nazi girls dress?

Anna   Fifties tea dresses?

Eireni   Maybe they dress normal.

The right-wing gangs at my high school, they were mostly boys. I'm trying to think how the girls dressed.

I think they wore band hoodies?

Anna   If I bleached my buzzcut and just left off any communist or anarchist gear, do you think I'd be all right?

We're really flirty but we haven't kissed.

Eireni   We haven't done anything – held hands or anything – that definitely confirms this is a date. And I'm just,

I'm aware of that.

Let's try and see if we can buy something.

Anna   What about that polyester shirt with all the flowers, that and a handkerchief over my head and I'd be away, right?

Jana *helps* **Anna** *put the shirt on.* **Jana** *buttons it up.*

Anna   The thing is I don't want anyone to think I'm a fascist.

Eireni   The whole point is to make them think you're a fascist!

Anna   Yeah but –

Ugh.

Imagine people thinking you're a fascist, though.

Eireni   We need to take this seriously or we will be fucked.

(And even at that moment I'm not thinking, I'm not sure at all we'll go through with this.)

Anna   (Me neither. You seem into it. You grew up in a place where there were right-wing gangs at school. You're brave and you have to be brave.)

Men love me, men have always loved me, they trust me right away.

Eireni   Really? They don't hate you?

Anna   I have this theory that they know I'll never break their heart. That what they can see –

that what they see right away is all they'll ever see.

Obviously there are dickheads everywhere but yeah, they trust me, lots of them.

Eireni   I want to kiss you, not exactly because I actually want to but just to confirm, you're mine, you're here for me.

You keep moving through the aisles of the shop as if you've somehow failed to read my mind.

Anna   You kiss me in this weirdly determined way but then we're kissing, we're kissing in front of the shop assistant, your hips twist towards me and my fingers are on the small of your back and yes, this feels like

in front of the shop assistant

maybe this isn't an experiment.

Eireni   Melt.

And then I put my hand on your chest but you have breasts which I'd – forgotten? – or, just not accounted for, so I basically just GRAB YOUR BOOB, WHYYY, I laugh, I fucking pray you laugh too.

Anna   I laugh! It's funny!

Eireni   The shop assistant also laughs which I could live without.

Anna   He puts up a fist. 'Baby dykes will save the world!'

Eireni   It seems like he's gay.

Anna   We go to a bar across the street called Grandmother's Medicine.

Eireni   This is the Northern sense of humour, I tell her, it's dry, no one is exactly laughing, but you know it's not serious.

Anna   Ha, dumb Southerners, actually wanting a laugh.

Eireni   No but –

this is

it's part of the city.

It's also part of the city.

We're not just a load of Nazis –

Anna   I know, oh my god, I know.

Eireni   This is where I'm from.

If I had to leave it would break my heart.

Anna   Do you think you might leave?

Eireni   No, no, it's just –

And I tell her. The sideways way my mum has of talking about Turkey. She doesn't talk about it much. The words are so much smaller than the loss.

Oh god, what rubbish talk.

Anna   This is your chance to try again.

For three days, Friday Saturday Sunday, you can be someone else.

Eireni   I've been thinking about it. It's got to be something similar, so I think you should be Annamaria or whatever and I should be Irina.

Anna   Irina! That's good.

Eireni   I know, right?

Anna   And we both think – foreign, but in a white way. Nicely placeable without anyone having to ask.

Eireni   And I thought of a good second name – Slanic!

Anna   Oh! Cool.

Er,

I don't actually think I know your real second name –

Eireni   Saltzmann, sorry. So Slanic is –

Anna   Salty! Salty Irina.

Eireni   Exactly.

Anna   Irina Slanic, Salty Irina.

It's dangerous, yeah?

I mean it will be dangerous.

Or I mean –

Hopefully nothing bad will happen. But the danger is real.

Eireni   I know that. You really don't need to explain that to me.

Anna   I'm saying you don't need to go through with it.

(But I already know you'll go through with it.)

Eireni   (And I have a little shiver, as though I know, this is it –

this may be the last time to turn back.)

It was *on* my *doorstep*.

Literally –

I don't know how many chances you get. To try and stop it.

My mother, my brothers –

they don't pass like I do. And if one day, something –

Anna   Oh.

Eireni   Like if it got worse and then they –

Awful beat.

Anna   OK. So.

We're going.

Eireni   (Out loud. The scariest thing. So that's it, I have to go. I'm stuck.)

People went to Spain, didn't they?

Anna   Yeah, wait what/are you – ?

Eireni   People went to fight fascists in Spain, during the 30s?

Anna   Yeah.

Eireni   So we can go to the hills for a few days, fucking hell, we don't just let it happen.

Anna   We don't just let it happen.

You are so beautiful and I don't want to be disrespectful but you are so beautiful.

Eireni   You're alright I think.

I think you're alright.

Anna   We don't just – let it happen. This is our country too.

Eireni   That's it, that's it. We're stronger than we think.

Anna   I don't want to live in a place where there's just blood on the pavement in the mornings and no one knows what happened but everyone knows what happened.

Eireni   Fucking – YES! That – double – thing –

It's like living in a nightmare.

////

Music: Dvořák's 8 Slavonic Dances, Op. 46, Number 1 in C (Presto)

Anna   We're hitchhiking to the festival.

Eireni   Because why not go all out with the risky decisions, right?

Anna   I've gone for cutoff shorts and that floral polyester shirt. And hiking boots.

Eireni   Butch, but Festival Butch!

Anna   I've even thrown in a daisy flower crown.

Eireni   I'm wearing a kind of loose gauzy white dress.

We could be going to Primavera Sound.

Anna   We could be going to Roskilde.

And I wonder, the stream of young people in cars to the farm where the festival's happening, do the other drivers on the road know who they are? Do they know – how can they know – what they believe?

Eireni   I've never known why white supremacists like their weird coded messages so much – all those numbers and symbols and runes. Now, standing by the side of the road hitchhiking, I wonder if it's because they're a bit ashamed, or they just know their beliefs are indefensible and they don't want to talk about it with people who might pick them up in cars.

Anna   A car slows down.

Eireni   It's a sunny day, the sky's proper summer deep blue.

Anna   Three skinny boys with acne are in the car.

Eireni   They look so much alike I think they're triplets for a moment. Then I see: brothers. Between thirteen and eighteen if I had to guess.

They're leaning out the window. 'Where are you going?'

Anna   I say the name of the festival and feel this flicker of absolute shame.

Eireni   'So are we! We'll take you all the way!'

Anna   We pack into the back of the car with the littlest brother. It's expensive, you can see it's all brand new, the seats are real leather and you can smell,

in the sun,

you can really smell that the seat used to be something's skin.

Eireni   These kinds of boys make girls like us disappear.

'Where have you come here from? Are you competing in the events?'

Anna   Competing? Events? I thought it was a festival but obviously I don't show I'm surprised, I just say no.

The middle-sized one, Theo, is the most talkative. I jump in, responding to any question, and I realise that I don't want you to speak in front of these boys.

Eireni   Why?

Anna   I don't know.

It feels like it'll protect you, like if you just don't speak –

Eireni   I don't have an accent.

Anna   It's not – you obviously don't have an accent, it's like if you don't talk then somehow you're not really there. And they can't touch you.

Eireni   It's not a funfair!

Anna   You burst out with it and everyone looks at you.

Eireni   It's not a funfair! It's a competition! What are you competing in?

Anna   Tobias, the oldest one, is competing in archery and bareback riding. Theo is competing in archery as well. There's also wrestling and fighting with long staffs but these boys are too skinny, they don't have a chance against the big country boys who'll be coming to the festival.

Eireni   'What's your favourite band that's playing?'

Anna   Fuck.

Eireni   'My favourite is the Turkhunters!'

Anna   There's a fucking band called the fucking TURKHUNTERS? Is what I think. But what I say is: oh my god they got the Turkhunters?!

Eireni   I look at my shoes and I pray you don't look my way, I pray you don't try and reassure me or do some stupid –

Anna   Theo is really showing off for you. I forgot that quiet is probably exactly how they like their women.

Eireni   I have the exact same feeling.

Anna   Will we need anything for protection?

Eireni   (Why did you say that?)

'What would you need protection from?'

Anna   We're girls. We're on our own. We might not know anyone, we're new to the scene.

Eireni   'We'll protect you!' That's the littlest one.

Anna   But he's quite sweet, though.

But he is!

He's an idiot, he doesn't believe in my full humanity as a person, but that doesn't mean he's not sweet though.

Eireni   The boys are talking about how they want to move to the country. How they wish they lived on a farm. They live in a flat overlooking the river, their grandfather's an industrialist and their mother's a whore, she moves from man to man like it's nothing. If they lived in the country they'd be strong.

Anna   They talk like my grandpa. The way they talk about the country. Fresh milk and early mornings –

Eireni   They think they're unwholesome.

Anna   D'you reckon?

Eireni   Yeah. They think they're dirty and they wanna be clean.

Anna   They seem really into the idea of protecting us. Tobias promises it'll be the safest festival we ever go to. Everyone there is a gentleman with proper respect for womanhood.

Eireni   (Unlike, dot dot dot.

I bite my tongue and breathe deep.)

Anna   But they will keep us safe. Not a hair on our heads will be harmed.

Eireni   At this point, a little pinprick of danger – will they be expecting – something in return –? But you don't seem worried.

Anna   I'm not worried. I think I've got their measure.

Eireni   I'm worried we'll turn into the forest and they'll keep us there and murder us. Grow mushrooms off our corpses. Use our heads for footballs. Make us dig our own graves. Whatever this lot normally do.

Anna   I'm convinced they're garden-variety knobheads, calling their mum a whore inside the car she bought them.

Eireni   And my fear does not come true just yet because here we are, at the gates of the farm where the festival is.

Anna   We see a field with horses in it. And beyond that, the yurts.

////

Eireni   We promise the boys we'll join them in the field.

Anna   The farmer who let us in looked normal, just normal. His son who helped with the gate, normal.

Eireni   I didn't see them looking at us funny, did you?

Anna   I don't think so. I could be wrong. But I don't think so.

Eireni   So we're in! (*Postures – Charlie's Angels.*) Like an American film.

Anna   Nauseous staggering, we've just got out of a long hot car ride in summer. It just looks like a farm. There are yurts in a field they've left fallow, one of them is sort of in the place where the festival meets the forest. There are horses in a pasture. Archery targets, I can see them at the far end of a field. A stage near the house. It's a farm, a festival on a farm.

Eireni   Did you think there would be big banners with swastikas?

Anna   Yes!

Or something.

This is worse, this just looks normal.

Eireni   Part of me wants to hide in the yurts and part of me wants to start eavesdropping. But that's basically how I always am at festivals – it's so full-on, so loud, so many people, sometimes I want to hide.

Anna   I look at the crowd and I realise we are actually really well-positioned to be here.

Eireni   Loads of boys, loads of teenage boys, most of them too fat or too thin, hair too long or too short, beards sparse. Very very few women.

Anna   Some of the women are older, rawboned.

Eireni   Not older. Like forty.

Anna   Yeah, older than us.

Eireni   The women all have boys trailing them like puppies.

Anna   A few older men, too. A bit like the squat. Just a few guys who've clearly been fighting this battle forever, who've seen generations of activists come and go.

Jonasz would fit in here if he wanted to. And he's straight and white.

Eireni   There's great energy – it feels really weird to say – but it's actually just high-energy, excitement, it doesn't seem violent yet.

Anna   Maybe it won't be. It's not a demo, after all. They're not trying to intimidate anyone. They're on their home turf.

Eireni   There's a boy with a bad sunburn riding bareback on one of the horses and a bunch of others applauding him.

Anna   We've decided we're gonna pretend to be newbies, not that we could really do anything else, we're gonna say we've only just started waking up to the dangers of immigration and the power of the fatherland, which is great because that gives us an excuse to ask questions, it gives them an excuse to explain things to us.

Eireni   We go over to the horses' field – there's a smell of sausages in the air, of roasting onions and peppers – and you suddenly say 'I want to take a picture of you, let me take a picture of you' – why would you want a photo of me at this right-wing festival?

Anna   You're not sure, I can suddenly see in your face that you don't know me that well, you don't completely trust me –

Eireni   And you pull me round so you're facing the stage, it all happens so quick –

Anna   Smile!

Eireni   And then you show me the photo, you've zoomed in so I'm not in the photo at all but the logos of the sponsors are, the far-right party, whoever's paying for it –

You look at me, as if to say, obviously.

And I feel a bit ashamed.

Anna   This will be much harder if we don't properly trust each other. I don't say that, we're weaving through a crowd, but I think it.

And I wonder why it's so easy for you not to trust me. If I shouldn't trust you.

Ugh, this is pointless, this is pointless.

Eireni   Tobias!

Anna   Tobias, the oldest brother from the car, he's on horseback now.

Eireni   He has a narrow back. His muscles are like whipcords.

Anna   Apparently shirtless horseback riding is the thing now for young Nazis.

Eireni   His shoulder blades remind me of a bird. A little bird.

Anna   Bet he'd be fucked off if you said that to him.

Eireni   I don't care, I'm not gonna say it to him, am I?

Being ashamed doesn't make me feel any warmer towards you, I notice.

Anna   There's a different current in the air since you saw the shirtless boys riding.

We haven't talked about whether you're gay or bi or even straight, fucked-up, closeted. We've just kissed.

Eireni   Have you ever ridden a horse?

Anna   No.

Wait, once I think. In a petting zoo when I was small.

Eireni   I never have. I'm scared of them.

Tobias!

Anna   Tobias!

And he winks at me but not at you.

Eireni   I think it's because I make him shy.

Anna   . . . Sure.

I send the photo of the logos to some of the squat people. Just in case.

Eireni   Just in case.

Anna   I'm gonna get punch, do you want punch?

Eireni   I'm going with you.

Anna   . . . OK.

Eireni   And as we leave the crowd I say – I think we need to stick together.

Anna   Yeah.

Yeah, that makes sense.

This punch is like 90 per cent homemade schnapps.

Eireni   Oh fuck, this punch is a problem . . . why would you give this stuff to a crowd of fifteen-year-olds?

Anna   The sun is beating down and we find some shade under a beech tree.

Eireni   We sip the punch. Supermarket syrup and moonshine.

Anna   Tobias wanders past and crawls under the tree next to us. He's still not wearing a shirt.

Don't you want to watch the others?

Eireni   'Others don't matter, do they? I've already got my marks. Just have to wait now.'

He sips my punch and I remember the thing I was afraid of, the thing where he protects us, and in return . . .?

Anna   'I love the country! I love being in the country! Look at this tree!'

Eireni   We look at the tree.

Anna   'There's enough space here, you know? People can just – live because they're not crowded in with anyone else. Not living in stacks on top of each other. Just – in the country – with enough light, and air.'

Eireni   And space.

Anna   'And space, yeah! Totally.'

He stares up into the branches, blissed out.

Eireni   We don't know what to talk about now he's here.

Anna   Is she straight? Obviously not. But does she think she's straight?

Eireni   Do they know? Do they know I'm an immigrant's daughter? Can everyone tell I'm not white? Why would you feed punch like this to a load of fifteen-year-olds in the middle of nowhere?

Do you want to go somewhere?

Anna   Where?

Eireni   Like the yurts or . . . somewhere?

This is . . .

I just wanna go somewhere.

Anna   Yeah. Let's explore.

It suddenly feels crazy to me that we would be here to find out more about the murders. Who are we gonna ask? The lost boys all around, the misfits from a dozen local high schools, do they shoot down immigrants in cold blood?

But. Do they shoot down immigrants in cold blood?

Let's ask Tobias to come with.

Eireni   No!

Anna   But Tobias has already heard us.

Eireni   'Where do you want to go?'

Anna   Irina wants to lie down. The punch and the heat.

Eireni   'Oh sure, sure sure sure! Yeah I can find you a place, my cousin was saying that yurt by the forest is all set up with stacks of bottles of water, like stacks on stacks, all the water for the whole camp is there, you can rest there, here I'll show you –'

He keeps going like that.

Anna   You look furious. But he's taking us where we want to go. He keeps spinning his phone in his hands and the case has a picture of Hitler on it.

I think about pink triangles. The ones that went before. We need to get information or this whole thing is a stupid risk for no reason.

Have you heard about the murders? The ones in the city?

Eireni   'There's always loads of murders in the city.'

Anna   The ones where immigrants keep getting shot, with no one else in their shops, no weapon left behind.

Eireni   'Really? I haven't heard about that.'

Anna   He seems genuinely curious. 'Maybe it's the Turkish Mafia. Sometimes they kill their own.'

Eireni   The victims weren't Turkish.

Anna   'So, what do you think happened?'

Eireni   Is this a trap?

I don't know what happened.

But it seems like us, doesn't it?

Anna   Something passes over Tobias' face. Pride, or –

Eireni   Not even pride. Just a little shiver.

Anna   'Yeah. It does seem like us.' US.

Eireni   How would we.

We're girls.

No one would suspect us.

How would we,

if we wanted to,

defend the fatherland,

how would we –

'Have you ever shot a gun?'

Anna   Yes.

We shoot rabbits where I'm from. I'm quick. I'm handy.

Eireni   I used to get into fights, we would fight the Turks on the beach in – (and I tell him the name of a town a few towns over from my town, so as not to – if there's someone here from my hometown) –

Do you know who,

who we'd talk to or –

Anna   'I don't know anything about anything like that.'

Eireni   Oh.

Cool.

Anna   'But I know someone,

I know, maybe,

someone who, I think might be able to help you.

I mean I don't know.'

Eireni   Yeah I mean us neither but –

Anna   'There are a lot of people here who get into fights.

What you're talking about is different.

You're talking about taking it to the next level.'

Eireni   Are we giving him ideas, are we actually feeding the far right here, and on the other hand fuck there are police spies here, he could be, anyone could be a police spy.

But we have to –

Anna   'You rest up in here.'

Eireni   We're in a yurt, shady, half-filled with crates of water bottles.

Anna   'I'm gonna go get someone. OK? And we'll figure it out.'

////

A long silence.

Eireni   It smells like turned earth.

My head is still spinning from the punch.

What did we do?

A silence.

Anna   I don't know.

. . .

I don't know.

Eireni   I think that was the wrong strategy.

I think we need to be prepared not to find out what happened.

Or they'll think we're cops.

Or the actual cops will find us.

What if someone from home is here?

Anna   Someone from –

Eireni   My town. My hometown.

What if someone recognises me?

Anna   Your hometown is on the coast, it must be 400 kilometres from here.

Eireni   These people travel. Not the ordinary ones, but the organisers, the hardcore ones, they travel.

Anna   Well don't freak out.

Eireni   Oh, fuck off.

Anna   I'm sorry but we need to – try and keep a grip and –

Eireni   Do you think they know?

Do you think they can tell?

Anna *softens.*

Anna   . . .

I don't think so.

There's absolutely no reason to think so.

Have some more water.

Eireni   That was a huge mistake.

Talking about the murders like that was a huge mistake.

. . .

Have you ever been beaten up for being gay?

Anna   No.

I've been chased down the street.

I've been spat at.

This fella got his dick out but maybe that was just a girl thing, not a gay thing.

One of my best friends stopped speaking to me when I came out.

But actually . . . some of the other girls stopped speaking to her, then. They made fun of her.

Eireni   Have you always known?

Anna   Er . . .

(and I'm aware I don't know, what you think you are, I don't know)

I went to Catholic school.

Not for, just because most of the schools are Catholic where I'm from.

I haven't always known . . . what being gay . . . is?

I used to wank to nothing, my best friends and I would talk about what we wanked about and for me it was nothing, just completely blank until I was about sixteen.

But I think my parents have always known?

Beat. **Anna** *spins around, goading herself.*

Anna   What about you?

Eireni   What about me what?

Oh –

. . .

Yes.

Yes I've always known I think.

Anna (*this is a very consequential question. Elaborately casual*)
Are you gay then?

Eireni   No.

That kind of thing doesn't make sense to me. Gay. Straight.
Like nothing against it but it makes no sense to me at all.

I've never understood how you can not fancy someone
because of their gender. If I'm honest. It makes no sense to
me at all.

Anna   Do your parents know?

Eireni   Probably not.

Anna   You suddenly empty a water bottle over your head.

Eireni   It's too hot! It's too –

Anna   You dump a water bottle at me.

Eireni   Look where we are, look where we are, I want to –

I kiss you.

I'm a virgin. Not that it matters.

I kiss you.

Anna   There's a feeling that a thunderstorm could be near.

Eireni   I want more punch, I want more –

Anna   You run your fingers on my thighs, it's a bit awkward, it's the same feeling as before, you need to prove it's sexual, you need to be sure –

Eireni   Your hair, I fuzz your hair, I've been wanting to rub your fuzzy head since I first saw you –

Anna   The smell of your skin.

Eireni   Your hair, your hairline, the nape of your neck.

Anna   Your teeth, your breasts.

Eireni   Your breasts, your waist. Your navel.

Anna   The impossible shape of your eyes.

Eireni   The rhythm of your breath.

Anna   Cicadas going silent, distant thunder. The perfect silence of every living thing apart from you.

Eireni   Afterwards we'll wash ourselves with bottled water.

Anna   We'll run around to dry.

Eireni   Turned earth. You look like a sculpture of a goddess, how can anyone be like you, how do you exist just walking around being yourself.

Anna   Your soft hair.

Eireni   The different colour of your pubes from mine. The different shape of your breasts, of your hips.

The different way hair sprouts from your face. Or maybe it's the same. The different smell of you.

Anna   Wetness, there's a word, it's like light on water, you're like light on water.

Your nails are too long, your cuticles are picked-at and raggedy, but we can work around that.

We move together.

Eireni   So tender. Unbearable –

Anna   – just us –

Eireni   – agonising –

Anna   – I've got the world at the tip of my fingers –

Eireni   – I've got the world at the tip of my tongue,

I've got the world in my mouth.

A long breath.

Eireni   And to be here – here, in the middle of a field, in the middle of a far-right festival –

it feels for a moment like we can't be stopped.

It feels like queerness will just sprout and bloom, it feels like anywhere, anywhere –

we will win.

Eireni *is very sure and peaceful.*

Anna *is taken aback.*

Anna   Do you think so?

Eireni   . . .

Yes.

Do you not think so?

Anna *looks at her.*

Anna   . . .

I –

No.

Eireni   Really? Really you don't think so?

Anna   I just think – this is ours.

And it feels really powerful.

But –

It isn't enough, is it?

It's cool that we're here, just like we're, everywhere. We've always been everywhere.

But we only have actual rights to be us, to be us out, now, right?

So it's a bit – a bit funny, a bit cool –

Eireni   I lost my virginity, to a woman, in a far-right camp!

Anna   But yeah. The – powerful feeling, of being with you –

it disappears if we don't use it for something.

I just don't think it's enough.

Beat.

Eireni   I think it's enough.

I think it can be enough.

Anna *silently disagrees.*

Sound of thunder.

Heavy summer rain.

The world changes. They are not alone.

Jana   Hiiiiii ladies!

Jana, *who has been manipulating the action from the start, is suddenly visible to them. Roughly their age. A naturally powerful person. All smiles.*

Eireni   Uh – hello.

Jana   I'm Jana. You guys are – Annamaria and Irina, right?

Anna   Yeah yeah!

Jana   Tobias sent me!

Anna   Yeah!

Jana   Where are you from? You've come from the city I know but –

Let me guess.

I feel like you're not from far.

And you – are you from the south?

Are you from one of the spa towns?

Anna   Oh my God, how did you do that?

Jana   I've got a gift, I just know, I've got a gift.

Eireni   We're – here to talk about –

Jana   AH ta ta ta ta let's,

I need to know who I'm talking to first don't I?

(*To* **Anna**.) Love your hair by the way.

I brought schnapps.

Anna   Awesome.

Jana   Yeah thought you might be getting a bit dry out here.

Is it possible this is an innuendo?? No, right?

Anna *drinks to cover her confusion.*

Jana   So you're from this neck of the woods.

You'll have seen how hard things are for the indigenous working class for your whole life, probably.

Eireni (*lying well*)   Yeah.

Jana   What is it that made you decide to come?

Eireni   It – just feels like –

it's getting to a critical point.

It's getting to a point where you have to choose a side.

Isn't it?

Jana   Completely.

Completely.

What about you, Annamaria?

Anna   Kind of the same, to be honest.

Jana   Irina, you're not drinking.

Eireni   It's so hot, I feel sick.

Jana   Annamaria is drinking and she's wearing that horrible shirt, that doesn't look very breathable does it? You must be very hot.

Anna   I'm all right.

Jana   Irina, you don't mind my asking, are you originally from here?

Because you look a bit like a Muslim.

Sure you don't want a drink?

Eireni *drinks*.

Eireni   I'm not Muslim, my family's from Serbia.

Jana   Serbia! Amaaaazing! Very underrated skiing in Serbia, I've heard, are you from the mountains?

Eireni   Yeah.

Jana   Really interesting time in Serbia right now, really interesting politically, do you ever think about going back?

Eireni   No. This is my home.

Jana   You should think about it really, there's a lot to learn from our people there, they've been so incredibly successful, we really have a lot to learn from them I think. Here, have some more.

Anna   Have some more water, Irina.

Jana   THANKS MUM! Does she need your permission then?

Eireni *takes a drink of schnapps.*

Jana   How did you get here?

Eireni   We hitchhiked. With Tobias.

Jana   Hmm. So you don't have a vehicle?

Uh huh.

Have you ever stolen one?

Anna   No but I bet it's not hard.

Doesn't look hard.

Jana   I like your style, Annamaria.

Jana *offers more schnapps.*

Jana   Let's play a game. Get to know each other.

Never have I ever – stolen anything.

Eireni *and* **Jana** *drink.*

Jana   Really! I would not have guessed to look at you! What have you stolen?

Eireni   I used to steal makeup all the time.

Anna   Really? Why?

Eireni   Erm –

I wasn't allowed to wear it?

So I just stole it?

Just to have and look at?

Jana   That's good though, security in pharmacies is way tighter than hardware stores and that, if you can steal makeup you can steal anything I reckon.

Ahem.

Never have I ever – kept a secret. Even from my nearest and dearest. Kept completely shtum.

They all drink.

Jana (*addressing both of them*)   You're good at keeping secrets then?

Eireni (*very casual*)   If I need to be.

There's something about the way she says this that makes **Anna** *nervous.*

Jana   Never have I ever been angry at my parents because they sold out our generation and trashed the planet and barely even noticed.

Everyone *drinks.*

Eireni   Never have I – wondered what it would have been like to have lived under Communism,

because maybe there'd be more opportunities, more equality for people like me,

but I don't know maybe there wouldn't.

Everyone *drinks.*

Anna   Really, you've wondered that?

Jana   I think we all wonder that. Now and again.

Anna   Never have I ever – felt, panic, over our economic system destroying our climate.

Jana   I actually –

sorry.

I don't really need to know about your feelings.

I need to know what you've done. And what you might do. So –

Never have I ever broken a window on purpose.

Jana *and* **Anna** *drink.*

Jana   Never have I ever drawn graffiti.

Everyone *drinks.* **Jana** *is pleased.*

Jana   Been arrested.

Anna *drinks.*

Jana   Oooh, really babe?

Anna *clocks why this is a bad answer.*

Anna   It wasn't – a big deal – it was vandalism –

Jana   But they have your fingerprints, yeah?

A bit of a crunchy silence.

Jana   Never have I ever had sex. (*They look at her quizzically.*) The boys'll want to know.

Jana *and* **Anna** *drink but* **Eireni** *does not.* **Anna** *is visibly surprised and hurt.* **Eireni** *quickly drinks.*

Jana (*amused*)   Forgot something, Irina?

Eireni   Ha! Erm –

Anna (*quickly*)   Never have I ever –

Hurt anyone, physically.

Jana *and* **Anna** *drink.* **Anna** *notices* **Jana** *drinking.* **Jana** *notices* **Anna** *noticing her drinking. To cover her confusion:*

Anna   What, you've never stepped on anyone's toe, you never got in a fight with your brothers, you've never hurt anyone, physically?

Eireni (*remembering*)   Oh. Yeah. I have!

Eireni *laughs and drinks.*

Jana   A bit of a mess, isn't she, Annamaria?

Thought Serbians were meant to be able to hold their liquor.

Eireni   It's hot, I'm losing track of the game a little bit.

Jana   Why don't you do the next one then.

Eireni   Never have I ever.

. . .

Caused – someone's – death.

*Silence. It feels as if anything might happen. Then **Jana** starts to laugh.*

Jana   Oh my god, are you serious?

What an unbelievably weird thing to ask!

*She puts aside the schnapps for now. **Eireni** feels bit as if she's tripped over the most popular girl in school or something.*

Eireni   Yeah. Yeah! Sorry . . .

Anna (*sees she needs to save the situation*)   I hate it.

You just see them growing, every day, don't you.

And I'm just supposed to not notice, how fucking ugly they are, not notice who's grabbing my arse on the train, not notice the fucking smell of their food, I hate it. I hate it.

Jana (*quietly, thoughtfully*)   Yeah.

Anna   I wouldn't have thought I'd ever come to something like this,

like I'm not from that sort of family or,

but they're so disgusting.

They disgust me.

Eireni *has been listening to this and no longer knows what to think.*

Jana   I think if you feel that way then you've come to the wrong place.

Beat.

Anna   Really?

Jana   Oh don't get me wrong, you can find people who feel like that. All over this festival I should think.

But if that's how you feel, you have no long-term future with this movement.

Anna   How. How should I feel.

Jana *likes the submissiveness of this question.*

Jana   Disgust burns fast.

Maybe you'll vote with us, but you won't be up to much in the streets, you'll burn out.

Disgust is not what keeps people turning up day after day.

Anna   What keeps people turning up?

Jana   Say you're feeling your disgust, you buy cigarettes at a cornershop, and you want this to be the last of our money the shopkeeper will ever take.

Hypothetically.

What's the first thing you need to ask yourself.

Anna   How do I get away?

Jana   Yes! Perfect. That is absolutely the first question you need to ask.

You need a safe escape route. So what would make it safe?

Anna   One where people wouldn't see,

people wouldn't be able to see you leave.

Jana   Yes! An unlocked, second exit.

Eireni   A silencer.

Jana   Yes that's good, but we're not talking about weaponry at the moment. We're talking about – selecting a target.

Anna   You'd need people who,

people with regular habits, people where you know where they're gonna be most of the hours of the day.

Jana   Yes. Exactly. Anything else?

Beat. They're thinking hard.

Eireni   A neighbourhood where you don't stand out.

Jana   Yes!

But also –

being a person who doesn't stand out.

Being a young woman who looks a lot like many other young women.

Maybe one with not such a trendy haircut, Annamaria.

Despite herself, **Anna** *is a bit gutted by* **Jana** *insulting her haircut. A beat.*

Jana   If a skinhead walks into a cornershop

everyone knows about it.

Everyone stands a little stiffer.

If a young woman walks in, everyone smiles.

Don't they?

The rain is quieting. There is a roar from the crowd.

Eireni   Is that fucking WONDERWALL?

Oh yes it is. Faintly.

Jana *passes the bottle round again.*

Jana   Think so.

Eireni   Fucking hell.

Jana   Do you not like Oasis?

Eireni   No it's,

this is weird, this has been a really weird day.

Jana   Have a bit more.

No really, it's from my granddad's garden, my granddad made it with peaches right off his trees, you'll insult my family if you don't have a bit more.

You know how I know Tobias?

His granddad fought with my granddad. In the war.

It was right at the end, they were both so young. Younger than us.

That's why our movement is strong. That's what keeps people turning up, day after day. It's love.

I fucking love this country.

I fucking love my people. I'm ready to fucking sacrifice, I will give my blood and my flesh if I need to.

Annamaria, your granddad must have fought as well, right?

Anna   Erm –

Anna *looks at* **Eireni**.

Anna   I mean –

he was so young.

We don't really talk about it.

Jana   Ask him about it when you go home.

I mean it.

We need to know our real history, the history that only our elders can tell us, that gives us love and honour for what we did. For all we sacrificed.

Jana *takes out two objects: a lighter and a huge Bowie knife with a vaguely folkish-looking hilt.*

She lights a flame and holds it to the edge of the knife.

She moves the flame very slowly back and forth along the knife's edge.

She is sterilising and heating the blade.

Jana   There is another thing.

Something that needs to happen if you want to know what happened to those poor shopkeepers.

I need to put the mark on you.

Jana *licks her finger and touches the knife. Nearly hot enough.*

Eireni   What's happening?

Jana   There's a brand. We all have it.

Some people have tattoos but you can get them removed.

Eireni   Aren't your fingers hot on that lighter?

Jana   Asbestos fingers, me.

Eireni   Let's go outside, let's go outside.

Anna   Do you know who did it?

Jana   Yes.

No.

I'll only tell you if you get the brand.

Eireni   Anna – maria, just, let's just slow down here –

Anna   Where does it need to be?

Jana   The hip.

It's always the hip.

Eireni   Just let her pray, she's religious, just let her say a prayer and she can think and then –

Jana   A brand is forever. We'll always know who you are.

Eireni   Drink some water, drink some more schnapps, your lighter is melting.

Jana   Irina, maybe you should take a walk, maybe have a breather outside, you're fucking with the vibe a little bit.

Anna   Show me your brand.

Jana   Fine.

Jana *rolls down her waistband.*

Anna   It doesn't look like much.

Jana   It got infected. That's why I'm being so careful with yours.

Anna   Are there any other initiation rituals?

Jana   There's one but you don't want to do it, trust me.

Anna   What is it?

Jana   I promise you don't want to do it.

Anna   Tell me.

Jana   You – have sex with a leader. You don't get to choose who.

Anna   What is it?

What is the shape – meant to be?

Jana   A double S.

Anna   SS?

Jana   Yeah.

Beat.

Anna   You'll tell me who did it?

Eireni   Don't be an idiot, Anna.

Jana   I will.

Eireni   She won't, Anna.

Anna   People need to be brave.

Eireni   How will you guarantee you'll tell her?

Jana   It's not even a big deal.

It's nothing.

That's why.

Anna   Do it. Do it quickly.

Eireni *dumps water over* **Jana** *and the burning knife.*

Jana   Jesus, what the fuck is wrong with you?

Eireni   Get out of here.

There's two of us and one of you. Get out of here.

Are you gonna slice us up in your yurt?

If all that comes from today is it's a tiny bit harder for Nazis round here because some psycho bitch fucked up some students at a festival that is *fine by me*.

Do it, the knife's in your hands, do it.

Jana *smiles.*

Eireni   She dropped the knife –

Anna   No,

no,

Eireni   She dropped the knife,

And touched the lighter to your shirt.

Jana *unbuttons* **Anna***'s shirt, from behind, almost embracing her. Then she is gone.*

Eireni   It went up like nothing.

It went up like a puddle of petrol.

You were screaming –

no,

it was like nothing (I'd ever heard),

it was not screaming,

it was like *nothing* –

Your hair,

it caught,

you rolled,

you were practical every second, you rolled in the wet dirt,

you were raw like a baby bird that's fallen out if the nest and can't get up.

You were so cold.

Earth in your wounds, shock,

like I didn't really know why it was called shock till I saw you with your half-burned head and your little arms there in the earth.

I want to cover you with something,

all I have is my dress so I –

we need to get you to the car,

what car?

I scoop you up and I shove as many bottles of water as I can in each arm and we're off,

Because I don't know how,

but right now, we absolutely have to steal a car.

////

We leave the hyperreality of the yurt for the unadorned reality of the stage.

We may suddenly be aware that **Anna**'s *been wearing a hat the whole show.*

She rubs her head and arms without thinking.

A totally different rhythm from the rest of the play.

Eireni *wants to put a good face on.*

Anna *wants to not be in pain.*

Canyons of silence.

Eireni   Anna was right to be honest, yeah, it's pretty easy to steal a car.

*This is a nervous attempt at a joke but **Anna** is silent.*

Eireni   You should.

Be more worried probably.

Most of you who have cars.

Anna *does not speak and therefore **Eireni** does not speak.*

Eireni   Stealing a car's not hard.

(*Trying to show **Anna** she understands.*) Physio's HARD.

Skin grafts are HARD.

Stealing a car? Sneaking into a far-right festival? Piece of piss.

Anna *does not speak.*

Eireni   Say something, say something.

Anna   I'm sorry.

. . .

I don't know what to say. I'm sorry.

Eireni   You shouldn't be/sorry –

Anna   OK but I AM sorry, OK.

It hurts even in my dreams.

Eireni   I know.

Anna   I don't want to talk about this now.

Eireni   I'm sorry.

Anna   Don't be sorry, so fucking useless, stop saying those useless words.

(*Clearly addressing the audience.*) A fire, when it's burning on your skin,

as long as it feels like it's burning it's because it is burning, if you can feel it burning it means you are still sustaining tissue damage even though the fire is technically 'out', it's still burning in your flesh, and I still feel it burning,

and I know it sounds like I'm making an analogy or something but I promise I'm not, I'm just trying to tell you what it's like inside my body, I just want you to know.

Silence.

Anna   You were very brave.

Eireni   Shut up.

Anna   No you were I'm serious. You were the reason it wasn't all a waste.

Tell them.

Eireni   It was the thing that she said about love.

We reported her to the police obviously.

Anna   And the police did nothing obviously.

Eireni   Yeah but I still think it was the right thing to do.

She was right.

A movement is built by love.

A movement is built by turning up every day, that's what love is, you turn up every day.

So that's what we do here, now.

Anna   Not 'we'.

Eireni   You, have been healing.

But the rest of us, the whole squat, the neighbourhood, when the shops close, the stu-dents, the retirees, the kids after school, anyone who's around, we all gather round the shops at closing time.

Because we're not gonna lose anyone else. No one. No one.

And it works. We haven't lost anyone since it started.

This is our home.

This neighbourhood, this city, this country is our home. You can't tell us different.

But I have to tell you something: every single day at closing time I don't want to turn up!

Every day I would rather do literally anything else!

It would be so easy not to show up, and I think about it every day, but I drag myself here anyway, every single day, because that is actually what love is, you just keep turning up, and that is actually what meaningful political action is, it's not swashbuckling your dumb-fuck way into a far-right camp, it's finding your people and showing up for them and that is boring as fuck but it's the only way.

A beat.

Anna   I love it when she talks this way.

I wish – (I could be like her)

I wish – (I could be like I was)

Eireni *waits for* **Anna** *to speak.*

But **Anna** *does not speak.*

Eireni *is uncomfortable, as if* **Anna***'s gone a bit off script.*

Anna*'s embarrassed her in front of people.*

Anna   One thing I did do.

I finished the sauna.

the thing –

people from the neighbourhood use it.

You didn't used to see people from the neighbourhood in the squat and now you do all the time.

Cause of the sauna.

And that –

yeah.

That makes me feel like this city,

it has problems,

but it's where I want to live.

Silence. **Eireni** *makes an abortive gesture, as if to touch her.* **Anna** *doesn't notice.*

They are not in the same place.

But **Anna** *is here with us. She knows what she wants to say.*

Anna   We should prepare for a good future, I think.

It will help us.

A beat.

Eireni   We need to be ready.

Music: Dvořák's 8 Slavonic Dances, Op. 46, Number 1 in C (Presto)